THINK RICH, LIVE FREE

THE PSYCHOLOGY OF FINANCIAL SUCCESS

RAJESH NAWAGEKAR

ISBN
Paperback 979-8-89744-954-5
Hardcase 979-8-89906-275-9

Contents

Part 3: Relationships and Money

Part 4: Practical Financial Tools

Acknowledgements

I express my deepest gratitude to my wonderful parents, Ashok Nawagekar and Ratan Nawagekar, for their unwavering guidance, blessings, and the values they instilled in me. Their support has been a cornerstone of my journey.

To my brother, Shailesh Nawagekar, and my sister-in-law, Smita Nawagekar, thank you for always being there with your unconditional support and encouragement. Your belief in me has been a constant source of motivation.

I extend heartfelt thanks to all my mentors, whose teachings and guidance have shaped my thoughts and efforts. Your wisdom has been invaluable in helping me navigate this journey.

This book is a testament to the support, love, and knowledge that I have been fortunate to receive from each of you.

Foreword

Money is not just about what you earn—it's about what you believe. In this transformative book, Rajesh Nawagekar challenges conventional wisdom about wealth and success, inviting you to reshape your financial mindset and take control of your future.

With years of expertise in investments and a deep understanding of how emotions and beliefs influence personal growth and financial success, Rajesh uncovers:

- The hidden money beliefs that may be holding you back—and how to break free from them.

- How to cultivate a wealth mindset that naturally attracts abundance.

- Practical financial strategies to manage, grow, and sustain your wealth.

- The powerful connection between relationships and financial well-being—and how to align both for lasting prosperity.

This book is more than just financial advice—it's a roadmap to breaking old patterns, achieving financial freedom, and rewriting your money story once and for all.

True wealth begins in the mind. Let this book guide you toward the abundant and fulfilling life you deserve.

An essential read for anyone looking to master the art of wealth creation and financial well-being.

– Lavvina Bangera

Hotelier and Life Coach

Suggestion to My Readers

My book is designed for anyone looking to deepen their understanding of the emotional, psychological, and practical aspects of money. It goes beyond traditional financial advice by tackling limiting beliefs and emotions that may prevent financial success. Whether you're overcoming debt, building wealth, or navigating financial dynamics in a relationship, this book provides actionable strategies and insights to help you achieve lasting financial transformation.

To derive the best value from this book, I suggest the following approach:

1. **Read Through Once:** Begin by reading the book cover to cover. This will give you a holistic understanding of the concepts and strategies discussed.

2. **Highlight Key Points:** As you read, note the ideas and strategies that resonate most with your current situation. These highlights will serve as your personalized roadmap for growth.

3. **Focus on Implementation:** True change comes from action. Revisit each chapter individually and commit to implementing the specific steps outlined.

4. **Embrace Patience:** Financial transformation is a journey, not a race. Give yourself the time and space to implement changes

effectively. Remember, this is about creating a lasting shift in your relationship with money and achieving long-term financial well-being.

By approaching the book with intention and action, you'll not only deepen your understanding of money's emotional, psychological, and practical aspects but also transform your financial mindset, empowering you to create a happier and more abundant life.

Part 1

The Foundation

Chapter 1

Transforming Your Money Beliefs

"All money is a matter of belief." – **Adam Smith**

Our beliefs about money are powerful—often more powerful than we realize. They shape how we think about finances, manage money, and ultimately, experience financial success or struggle. Imagine your beliefs as a compass: they guide your decisions and shape your financial journey, whether you're aware of them or not.

However, many of us have limiting beliefs about money that can act as invisible barriers, preventing us from achieving our true financial potential. These beliefs, often ingrained in us since childhood, are the root cause of many financial struggles. It's time to recognize these beliefs, challenge them, and replace them with empowering thoughts that will transform your financial future.

Money Beliefs: How They're Formed

Our relationship with money begins long before we start managing our finances. Much of what we believe about money is formed during childhood, influenced by the people around us and the experiences we have. These foundational beliefs become the lens through which we view the world, and when it comes to money, they can either empower us or hold us back.

Example:

Many of us, especially in traditional Indian households, have heard phrases like "Money doesn't grow on trees" or "A big house and car mean nothing if you don't have peace of mind." While these beliefs may be rooted in valuable lessons of humility, they can also create a mindset of scarcity, causing us to believe that money is difficult to earn or that it's inherently evil.

However, some grow up in more financially abundant environments, where ideas like "Hard work always brings wealth" or "There's always a way to make more money" are instilled. These positive beliefs can create a sense of possibility and motivation, empowering individuals to pursue financial success confidently.

The Role of Family and Trauma in Shaping Money Beliefs

1. **Family of Origin:**

   Your family's experiences with money deeply influence your beliefs. For example, if you grew up hearing stories about financial struggle or witnessed your parents constantly stressing over bills, you might develop beliefs like "Money is hard to come by" or "You have to sacrifice to make money." On the other hand, if your parents were financially successful, you might develop a belief that "making money is easy" or "wealth is a natural result of hard work."

2. **Trauma and Money Beliefs:**

   Our beliefs about money can also be shaped by past trauma. This could be something as severe as losing your home in a fire or a less obvious trauma, like being teased at school for wearing inexpensive clothes. These experiences create emotional reactions that influence how we manage money as adults.

- **Example:** If someone has faced financial hardship or loss, they may develop a hoarding mentality—fearful of losing everything again. This fear can lead to constantly saving but never investing or spending on things that could improve their quality of life.

- On the other hand, if you were mocked for your appearance or possessions as a child, you might develop an unhealthy attachment to material wealth as a means of protecting your self-worth.

Common Limiting Beliefs About Money

Here are some common limiting beliefs many of us unknowingly carry:

1. **Money is Evil or Dirty:**

   A belief that money is morally corrupt can make us feel guilty for wanting financial success. This belief can prevent us from pursuing wealth and building abundance.

2. **I'm Not Good with Money:**

   If you've made financial mistakes in the past, you might develop a belief that you're just "bad with money." This can lead to avoidance, procrastination, and financial instability.

3. **Money is Scarce:**

   The scarcity mindset, often formed through early experiences or economic instability, makes us feel that there's never enough. It can lead to hoarding, a fear of spending, and a reluctance to take risks.

4. **I Need to Be Rich to Be Happy:**

   Believing that wealth is the only way to happiness can create dissatisfaction even after achieving financial success. This belief can drive you to constantly chase more without ever feeling fulfilled.

5. **I'm Not Deserving of Wealth:**

   Negative self-beliefs can lead to self-sabotage. If you don't believe you're worthy of wealth, you might unconsciously push opportunities away or make poor financial decisions.

6. **Money Can Solve All Problems:**

   While money can alleviate certain challenges, it isn't the cure for everything. Overvaluing money can lead to unrealistic expectations and disappointment.

Below is the Detailed List of Other Limiting Beliefs

- Money is hard to earn.
- Rich people are greedy or selfish.
- You have to work extremely hard to make money.
- I'll never be financially free.
- I'll never earn more than I do now.
- Talking about money is rude or inappropriate.
- Money changes people for the worse.
- It's impossible to make money doing what I love.
- Saving money is more important than investing it.
- I don't deserve to earn more than others around me.
- Financial success will make others jealous of me.
- Managing money is too complicated for me to learn.

- I'll lose all my money if I try to invest.

- My family has always struggled financially, so I will too.

- Money isn't important; passion is all that matters.

- Making money is stressful.

- Only certain types of people become wealthy.

- Money corrupts creativity or passion.

- I'll never get out of debt.

- Financial success is a matter of luck, not effort.

- I need advanced education or credentials to make good money.

- People like me don't become rich.

- If I become wealthy, people won't like me anymore.

- Making a lot of money means sacrificing your personal life.

- If I give away money, I'll lose what I need.

- Money causes more problems than it solves.

- Having wealth is risky because I could lose it all.

- I'm too young/old to achieve financial success.

- There's not enough money in the world for everyone to succeed.

- It's selfish to want more money when others have less.

- Being wealthy requires unethical behavior.

- I need to take big risks to make money.

- I should always prioritize others' financial needs over mine.

- Financial success means giving up personal values.

- I'll never be able to retire comfortably.

- If I don't struggle, I won't value my money.

- I can't make money without a traditional job.

- Money always causes conflict in relationships.
- Spending money on myself is wasteful or indulgent.
- I'm not smart enough to handle large sums of money.
- Financial freedom is only for the lucky few.
- Money is a source of constant worry.
- You have to choose between wealth and happiness.
- Rich people don't have true friends.
- I need someone else to manage my finances for me.
- Earning more money means having less time for family and friends.
- I'll never have enough money to live the life I want.
- People will judge me if I have too much money.
- I'll be trapped by my wealth.
- Success and financial security are incompatible.

Breaking Free from Limiting Money Beliefs

It's possible to rewrite your financial story and replace limiting beliefs with empowering ones. Here's how you can start today:

1. **Engage in Positive Self-Talk:**

   To transform your money beliefs, you need to replace negative thoughts with positive affirmations. For example, if you've been holding onto the belief that "making money is difficult," replace it with "making money is easy and enjoyable."

   Say these affirmations regularly to create a better money mindset

   - *"I am worthy of financial success."*
   - *"Money flows to me easily and consistently."*
   - *"I am in control of my financial destiny."*

2. **Practice Gratitude for Your Finances:**

Gratitude is one of the most powerful tools for transforming your financial mindset. No matter how much or how little you have, be thankful for it. This mindset shift can move you from scarcity to abundance, attracting more prosperity into your life.

Example: Begin your day by writing down three things you're grateful for about your financial situation, whether it's your steady income, savings, or even the lessons you've learned from past financial mistakes.

3. **Seek Financial Education:**

Empower yourself with knowledge. Learn the basics of budgeting, saving, investing, and debt management. Knowledge is power, and the more you understand about personal finance, the more confident you will feel about making smart financial decisions.

Action Steps:

- Read books or attend workshops on personal finance.

- Join communities focused on financial literacy.

4. **Replace Old Beliefs with New Ones:**

Identify your limiting beliefs, and consciously replace them with new, empowering beliefs. For example, if you've believed "I'll never be rich," replace it with "I am capable of creating wealth." Repeat these new beliefs daily and visualize yourself living them.

How to Do It: Write your new money beliefs on paper, say them out loud, and display them in visible places around your home. The more you see and hear them, the more likely they are to be accepted by your subconscious mind.

5. **Take Action: Small Steps Lead to Big Changes:**

   Action is the key to reinforcing your new beliefs. Start small—save a little more, invest a little more, and be mindful of your financial choices. As you see results, your confidence will grow, and your new beliefs will become your reality.

   Example:

   - Start a SIP (Systematic Investment Plan) with as little as ₹500 per month.

   - Review your spending and make a conscious decision to cut back on unnecessary expenses.

   - Build an emergency fund of ₹10,000—no amount is too small to start.

Conclusion: Your Financial Transformation Starts Today

The beliefs you carry about money have the power to shape your financial destiny. If you've been living with limiting beliefs, now is the time to break free from them. Start by identifying and challenging those beliefs, replacing them with empowering ones that align with your true potential. By taking consistent action—through gratitude, education, and positive affirmations—you will create a new financial reality for yourself.

Action Steps:

1. Engage in positive self-talk—replace limiting money thoughts with empowering affirmations and repeat them daily.

2. Identify your limiting beliefs and replace them with empowering beliefs.

3. Practice gratitude for the money you have and the abundance you're attracting.

4. Seek financial education to build confidence in managing your money.

5. Start small—take concrete steps towards improving your financial situation.

Call to Action

Your financial freedom is within your grasp, but it all begins with a single decision—transforming the beliefs that have held you back. Don't wait another day to start reprogramming your mindset. Take the first step towards a life of abundance and financial success right now. Identify your limiting beliefs, replace them with empowering ones, and commit to taking action. Your new financial future starts today—take control, believe in your worth, and unlock the wealth and freedom you deserve!

Chapter 2

The Role of Emotions in Financial Decisions

"If you cannot control your emotions, you cannot control your money."
– Warren Buffet

Our financial decisions are deeply intertwined with our emotions. Whether we feel excitement, fear, or anxiety, these emotions can profoundly shape how we save, spend, and invest. By understanding and managing these emotions, we can make choices that align with our long-term financial goals and avoid common pitfalls.

Why Emotions Matter in Financial Decisions

Imagine receiving an unexpected windfall. Would you splurge on a luxury item, save it, or invest it? Your decision might depend on your emotional state. Studies show that positive emotions like happiness often lead to greater financial risks, while negative emotions like fear can result in overly cautious decisions.

Example: Mike Tyson earned over $400 million during his boxing career, but his impulsive spending, fueled by emotions, led to financial ruin. From purchasing Bengal tigers to extravagant mansions, Tyson's lack of financial education and emotional regulation highlighted the

10

dangers of letting emotions dictate financial choices. Today, Tyson is a cautionary tale of the importance of balancing emotions with rational decision-making.

Understanding Emotional Triggers

Our emotions are often linked to deep-seated beliefs about money. Excitement may stem from associating wealth with freedom, while fear may arise from experiences of scarcity. Recognizing these triggers can provide valuable insights into our financial behaviors.

Ask Yourself: How often do your emotions influence your financial choices? Could you benefit from pausing to reflect before making decisions?

The Impact of Cognitive Biases on Emotions

Emotions are often amplified by cognitive biases, which act as mental shortcuts that can lead to flawed decisions. Here are three common biases:

1. **Overconfidence:** Believing you can outsmart the market.

   Example: Investing heavily in a single stock, assuming it will always perform well.

2. **Loss Aversion:** The fear of losing money outweighs the desire for gains.

   Example: Holding onto a declining asset because selling feels like admitting defeat.

3. **Anchoring: Relying too much on initial information.**

   Example: Refusing to lower the price of a property, even if market conditions have changed.

Deeper Insights: These biases often operate unconsciously, making them difficult to identify. Overconfidence might be driven by a desire for control, while loss aversion often reflects a fear of regret.

Action Steps:

- Reflect on recent financial decisions. Were they influenced by biases?

- Challenge your assumptions by seeking objective advice.

Question: Which bias do you find most influences your decisions, and how can you counteract it?

The "Fight or Flight" Response in Finance

When faced with a financial challenge, our natural "fight or flight" response often kicks in. Consider the following scenarios:

Fight: Using excitement from a financial windfall to make impulsive purchases.

Flight: Reacting to a market downturn by panic-selling investments.

Broader Implications:

The "fight or flight" response doesn't just affect individual decisions; it can influence entire markets. For example, widespread fear during a recession can lead to collective panic selling, exacerbating economic downturns.

Example: During the 2008 financial crisis, many investors sold their assets in fear. However, those who stayed calm and maintained their investments often saw significant recoveries in the years that followed.

Action Steps:

- Before making a decision, take a moment to breathe and evaluate your emotions.

- Seek guidance from a trusted advisor to bring objectivity to the situation.

Ask Yourself: How can you create a strategy to pause and reflect during financial stress?

External Factors: Social Pressure and Trends

Emotions are not only internal; external factors can influence them, like market trends or peer behavior. FOMO (Fear of Missing Out) often drives people to invest in trending assets without proper research.

Navigating External Pressures:

Understanding the influence of societal norms and media can help mitigate emotional reactions. For example, advertisements often use emotional appeals to encourage spending, while financial news might sensationalize trends to attract attention.

Example: The cryptocurrency boom saw many inexperienced investors jump in, driven by hype rather than understanding the risks. While some profited, many suffered losses when the market corrected.

Action Steps:

- Focus on your financial goals instead of external noise.

- Educate yourself about investment opportunities before committing.

Question: Are your financial decisions driven by your goals or influenced by others?

Managing Emotions for Financial Success

Building Emotional Intelligence:

Emotional intelligence is the ability to recognize, understand, and manage emotions. This skill is invaluable for financial success, as it allows you to navigate decisions with clarity and composure.

1. **Recognize Emotional Triggers:** Identify what causes emotional reactions in your financial life.

2. **Practice Emotional Regulation:** Develop techniques like deep breathing or journaling to manage stress.

3. **Rely on Data:** Base your choices on evidence rather than feelings.

Example: Warren Buffett's investment strategy emphasizes rationality over emotion. By staying calm during market fluctuations, Buffett has consistently made sound financial decisions.

Ask Yourself: What habits can you develop to make data-driven decisions?

The Gardening Analogy in Finance

Financial decision-making is like tending to a thriving garden. Each financial choice is a seed you plant, and with the right care, it has the potential to grow into something meaningful and sustaining. Just as gardeners prepare the soil, choose seeds carefully, and nurture their plants through seasons of change, effective financial planning requires thoughtful preparation, consistent attention, and patience.

Detailed Examples:

1. **Emergency Funds as Shrubs:** Imagine setting up an emergency fund. It's like planting a resilient shrub that can withstand storms. With consistent watering (regular contributions), it becomes a reliable source of security when unexpected challenges arise.

2. **Retirement Planning as Fruit Trees:** Planning for retirement is akin to growing a fruit tree. Small, regular investments in a retirement account (like tending to a sapling) will yield bountiful rewards in the future, providing sustenance and comfort for years to come.

3. **Diversification as a Variety of Crops:** Diversifying your investment portfolio is like planting a variety of flowers and crops. Some may flourish in different seasons, ensuring your financial "garden" remains vibrant and productive over time.

4. **Budgeting as Pruning:** Managing a budget is like pruning a garden. Regularly cutting back unnecessary expenses helps resources flow to areas that matter most, ensuring healthy growth.

Action Steps:

- Begin with a clear plan: Define your financial goals and outline actionable steps.

- Tend to your finances regularly: Monitor your budget and investments consistently.

- Be patient and adaptable: Recognize that growth takes time and adjust your strategy as needed.

Ask Yourself: Are you cultivating your financial garden with intention and care? What seeds can you plant today to ensure future prosperity?

Conclusion: Harnessing Emotions for Financial Growth

Emotions are powerful allies or adversaries in financial decision-making. By understanding their influence, we can channel them positively and avoid common traps. Cognitive biases, external pressures, and emotional impulses are part of being human, but they don't have to define your financial journey.

Action Steps:

1. **Pause Before Acting:** Recognize your emotional state and take a moment to reflect.

2. **Set Clear Goals:** Define your financial objectives and align your decisions with them.

3. **Seek Education:** Continuously learn about personal finance to build confidence.

4. **Develop a Support System:** Surround yourself with financial advisors and peers who encourage rational decision-making.

Call to Action

Mastering your emotions is the key to making sound financial decisions. Start by taking small, actionable steps: reflect on your emotional triggers, challenge your cognitive biases, and create a plan to pause and evaluate before making major financial choices. Surround yourself with resources, tools, and a support system to stay informed and grounded in your financial journey.

Take the first step today: Write down one emotional trigger and a strategy to manage it. Building awareness now will set the foundation for smarter, more intentional decisions in the future.

Chapter 3

Balancing Positive Emotions and Financial Decisions

*"In the world of money and investing,
you must learn to control your emotions ." – **Robert Kiyosaki***

Positive emotions, such as joy, excitement, and optimism, can inspire us to reach new heights. However, when not balanced with thoughtful financial decisions, these emotions may lead to impulsive actions or unrealistic expectations. In India, where celebrations like weddings, festivals, and personal milestones often involve significant expenses, learning to harness positive emotions is crucial for achieving financial security and well-being.

The Impact of Positive Emotions on Financial Decisions

Positive emotions influence financial behavior in profound ways. For instance:

- **Excitement and Enthusiasm:** May lead to impulsive purchases during festive sales or investments in high-risk schemes without due diligence.

- **Joy and Satisfaction:** Can encourage spending on activities or items that enhance quality of life but may sideline long-term goals.

- **Confidence and Optimism:** While beneficial, overconfidence can result in neglecting financial planning or underestimating risks.

Example: During Diwali, Ravi felt overjoyed after receiving his bonus. In his excitement, he purchased an expensive car without considering the long-term EMI burden. Recognizing such patterns is essential for making balanced financial choices.

Ask Yourself: How do positive emotions influence your financial decisions? Are your choices aligned with your long-term goals?

Strategies for Balancing Positive Emotions and Financial Decisions

1. **Acknowledge and Understand Your Emotions:**

   Recognize the emotions driving your financial decisions. Understanding these feelings can help you channel them effectively.

   Action Steps:

   - Reflect on the reasons behind your excitement before making a decision.

   - Ask yourself if your decision stems from sound reasoning or a temporary emotional high.

   Example: Priya, thrilled after a salary hike, planned a vacation but ensured she allocated funds for her Mutual Fund SIPs (Systematic Investment Plans) first.

2. **Set Clear Financial Goals:**

Having well-defined goals helps channel positive emotions into constructive actions.

Action Steps:

- **Short-Term Goals:** Save for festivals, vacations, or gadgets.

- **Long-Term Goals:** Plan for retirement, buying a home, or children's education.

Example: Arjun saved ₹5,000 monthly toward a down payment for his dream home while enjoying occasional dining out, maintaining a balance.

Ask Yourself: Do your financial goals reflect both immediate joy and future security?

3. **Create a Decision-Making Framework:**

Structure your financial decisions to minimize impulsive choices.

Action Steps:

- **Use a checklist:** Evaluate affordability, necessity, and alignment with your goals before making a purchase.

- **Follow the 24-Hour Rule:** Wait a day before making big purchases to make sure you're thinking clearly.

Example: Before investing in an expensive gadget during a sale, Kavita waited a day. She realized it wasn't a priority and redirected her funds toward her travel savings.

4. **Leverage Positive Emotions to Enhance Financial Health:**

Channel your enthusiasm into building good financial habits.

Action Steps:

- Turn budgeting into a rewarding activity by celebrating small wins.

- Use excitement to learn about new investment opportunities.

Example: Rohan's excitement after completing his first SIP installment motivated him to start another for his emergency fund.

5. **Balance Risk and Reward:**

Positive emotions may lead to overconfidence. Balance optimism with a realistic view of risks and rewards.

Action Steps:

- Evaluate investments for potential gains and risks.

- Diversify to spread risk and ensure stability.

Example: Meera balanced her excitement about the stock market by allocating 70% of her portfolio to mutual funds and bonds for safety.

Ask Yourself: Are you balancing your enthusiasm with informed risk management?

6. **Practice Mindfulness in Financial Decisions:**

Mindfulness helps you remain aware of both your emotions and financial reality.

Action Steps:

- **Practice Mindful Spending:** Assess if expenses align with your goals.

- **Develop Emotional Awareness:** Identify how joy or excitement might skew decisions.

Example: During a wedding shopping spree, Neha paused to consider her budget, ensuring her purchases didn't strain her finances.

7. **Celebrate Financial Milestones Wisely:**

Celebrations are important but should be planned thoughtfully to avoid financial strain.

Action Steps:

- Allocate a portion of your budget for milestones.

- Choose celebrations that are meaningful but within your financial means.

Example: Raj and Anjali celebrated their 10th anniversary with a budget-friendly vacation, saving the rest for their children's education.

Ask Yourself: How can you celebrate milestones without jeopardizing your financial goals?

8. **Educate Yourself Continuously:**

Use your enthusiasm to explore financial growth opportunities.

Action Steps:

- Attend workshops or read books by financial experts.

- Join communities focused on financial literacy and wealth building.

Example: After gaining investment knowledge from a book, Akash diversified his portfolio to include gold ETFs, ensuring both security and growth.

9. **Build a Financial Safety Net:**

A positive outlook may lead to overlooking potential challenges. Prepare for uncertainties with a robust safety net.

Action Steps:

- Create an Emergency Fund: Save at least six months of expenses.

- Get adequate insurance for health, life, and property.

Example: Shweta's emergency fund helped her manage unexpected medical expenses without dipping into her investments.

10. Balance Present Enjoyment with Future Security:

Ensure your plans reflect both current happiness and long-term goals.

Action Steps:

- Allocate resources for current pleasures while safeguarding the future.

- Review your financial plan regularly to accommodate changes.

Example: Anil balanced monthly entertainment expenses with disciplined investments in an NPS (National Pension Scheme) for retirement.

Conclusion: Harnessing Positive Emotions for Financial Growth

Balancing positive emotions with financial decisions is key to achieving joy and stability. By recognizing how your emotions influence decisions and employing thoughtful strategies, you can create a fulfilling financial journey.

Action Steps:

1. **Pause and Reflect:** Identify emotional triggers and align them with your goals.

2. **Plan with Purpose:** Develop clear short-term and long-term financial objectives.

3. **Educate Yourself:** Continuously learn to make informed decisions.

4. **Celebrate Thoughtfully:** Enjoy milestones without compromising future plans.

Call to Action

Take charge of your positive emotions today! Reflect on one recent financial decision influenced by excitement or joy. Was it aligned with your goals? Use the strategies shared in this chapter to harness your enthusiasm and create a balanced financial plan. Start small, stay consistent, and let your positive emotions propel you toward financial success.

Chapter 4

Balancing Negative Emotions and Financial Decisions

*"Money, like emotions, is something you must control to keep your life on the right track." – **Natasha Munson***

In India's vibrant and diverse culture, emotions and financial decisions often go hand in hand. Whether it's planning for a grand wedding, managing household expenses, or investing in gold, negative emotions like stress, anger, or anxiety can cloud judgment. This chapter explores how to balance these emotions with practical financial wisdom.

The Connection Between Emotions and Finances

In Indian households, emotions often drive financial decisions. For instance, the societal pressure to fund extravagant celebrations or provide for extended family can lead to financial strain. Conversely, financial struggles like mounting loans or unexpected expenses can intensify stress and anxiety.

Examples:

- **Stress and Anxiety:** Ignoring utility bills or EMIs due to feeling overwhelmed by monthly commitments.

- **Anger:** Impulsive online shopping during festive sales as a way to cope with frustration.

- **Family Expectations:** Prioritizing children's education or marriages over personal savings.

Ask Yourself: How do your emotions shape your financial decisions in a typical month? Are cultural pressures influencing your choices?

Strategies to Balance Emotions and Financial Choice

1. **Acknowledge Your Emotions:**

   In a culture where emotions are often intertwined with financial responsibilities, it's important to first acknowledge your feelings. Whether it's stress over paying off a personal loan or guilt for not meeting family obligations, recognition is the first step toward resolution.

   Action Steps:

   - Keep a journal to document your feelings about specific financial situations.

   - Discuss your emotions with trusted family members or friends for support.

   Example: Priya, a working mother, realized her anxiety stemmed from trying to meet both her children's tuition fees and her parents' medical expenses. Journaling helped her identify areas to prioritize.

2. **Separate Emotional Reactions from Financial Decisions:**

   Many Indians associate money with emotions like pride or guilt, often leading to reactive decisions. Take a step back to ensure your choices align with long-term goals.

Action Steps:

- Implement a 48-hour rule before making non-essential purchases, especially during sales like Flipkart's Big Billion Days or Amazon's Great Indian Festival.

- Create a checklist to evaluate large financial commitments, such as buying gold or property.

Example: Raj waited two days before booking a luxury vacation during a festive discount. This pause helped him realize he needed to prioritize his home loan repayment.

3. **Develop a Financial Plan:**

   A solid financial plan can ease emotional stress, providing clarity and control.

   Key Components:

   - **Budgeting:** Create a budget to track and manage your expenses effectively.

   - **Emergency Fund:** Save at least six months' worth of expenses to handle crises like medical emergencies.

   - **Investments:** Diversify with fixed deposits, mutual funds, and traditional options like gold or Public Provident Fund (PPF).

   Example: Sunita's financial plan included setting aside ₹10,000 monthly for her son's higher education. This goal reduced her stress and kept her spending in check.

4. **Practice Mindfulness and Stress-Reduction Techniques:**

   Yoga and meditation cultivate mindfulness by calming the mind and reducing stress, helping you stay present and centered in daily life.

Action Steps:

- Dedicate 15 minutes daily to deep breathing or yoga.

- Develop a meditation habit.

Example: Anil used meditation to calm his mind before reviewing his business finances, leading to more thoughtful decisions.

Ask Yourself: How can mindfulness techniques improve your financial clarity and focus?

5. **Seek Professional Guidance:**

Consult professionals for financial or emotional support. Don't hesitate to seek help when needed.

Who to Approach:

- **Chartered Accountants (CAs):** For tax planning and investment strategies.

- **Counselors/ Life Coaches:** To address emotional challenges related to financial stress.

- **Certified Financial Planners (CFPs):** For comprehensive financial planning.

Example: Ravi consulted a CFP to restructure his debt and create a SIP (Systematic Investment Plan), which eased his financial burden significantly.

6. **Enhance Financial Literacy:**

Understanding financial concepts is essential to navigate India's dynamic economic environment. From managing digital payments to selecting the right insurance plan, education empowers better decisions.

Action Step:

- Attend workshops or read books/blogs on personal finance.

Example: Meera attended a workshop on mutual fund investments, which helped her start an SIP and plan for retirement effectively.

7. Set Realistic Financial Goals:

Goals keep you motivated and focused, reducing feelings of frustration or helplessness.

Action Steps:

- Define short-term goals, such as saving ₹5,000 monthly for a festival fund.

- Outline long-term aspirations, like building a retirement corpus through EPF (Employee's Provident Fund) and NPS (National Pension System).

Example: Vinod's goal of saving for his daughter's wedding helped him cut unnecessary expenses and invest in gold ETFs systematically.

Conclusion: Mastering Emotions for Financial Harmony

Balancing emotions with financial decisions are essential in an emotionally charged and culturally rich environment like India. By acknowledging your emotions, creating a financial plan, and using mindfulness practices, you can break the cycle of stress and poor financial choices.

Action Steps:

1. **Reflect on Emotions:** Identify how cultural or familial expectations influence your financial behavior.

2. **Plan for Stability:** Develop a tailored financial plan that includes budgeting and saving for emergencies.

3. **Practice Mindfulness:** Use yoga or meditation to stay calm during financial decision-making.

4. **Educate Yourself:** Leverage resources to improve your financial literacy.

Call to Action

Take the first step in addressing your negative emotions today! Reflect on one recent financial decision driven by stress, fear, or frustration. Did it align with your goals, or was it reactive? Use the strategies from this chapter to pause, identify emotional triggers, and replace impulsive reactions with thoughtful planning. Start by implementing one mindfulness practice or financial strategy and gradually build toward emotional and financial harmony.

Part 2

The Wealth Mindset

Chapter 5

The Happy Millionaire Mindset

"Start with the end in mind. If you want to be a millionaire, talk like one, act like one, work like one."– **Bob Proctor**

Adopting a millionaire mindset is about more than just accumulating wealth—it's about creating a life that radiates happiness, fulfillment, and financial success. When you operate on the frequency of a happy millionaire, you unlock your full potential for both joy and prosperity. Here's how you can cultivate this mindset and achieve extraordinary results.

1. **Embrace Gratitude and Appreciation for What You Have:**

   Case Study: Tony Robbins advocates for daily gratitude practices. By focusing on the abundance in his life, Robbins has cultivated a mindset of joy and positivity that fuels his success.

   Key Lesson: Gratitude shifts your focus from lack to abundance, opening the door to happiness and wealth.

   Action Steps:

   - Start a gratitude journal. Each day, write down three things you're thankful for.

33

- Pause during challenges to reflect on the blessings you often overlook.

- Share your gratitude with others to strengthen relationships and foster positivity.

2. **Don't Seek Perfection:**

Case Study: Reid Hoffman, the co-founder of LinkedIn, famously said, "If you are not embarrassed by the first version of your product, you've launched too late." This highlights the importance of taking action rather than waiting for perfection.

Key Lesson: Perfectionism can paralyze progress. Embrace imperfection as a necessary part of growth.

Action Steps:

- Set realistic deadlines and stick to them, even if the result isn't perfect.

- Focus on progress over perfection. Celebrate small wins.

- Learn from imperfections to improve iteratively.

3. **Embrace Abundance Over Scarcity:**

Case Study: Sara Blakely, founder of Spanx, built her billion-dollar empire by rejecting the fear-based scarcity mindset. She believed there was plenty of room in the market for innovative ideas, and her success proved her right.

Key Lesson: Wealth isn't a zero-sum game. Abundance thinking creates opportunities for growth.

Action Steps:

- Replace limiting beliefs with affirmations like, "There is enough success for everyone."

- Focus on opportunities instead of competition.

- Celebrate others' successes as inspiration rather than threats.

4. **Believe in Your Worth and Value:**

Case Study: Sheryl Sandberg negotiated her salary at Facebook with confidence, understanding her value. This boldness ensured she was compensated fairly and set a precedent for others.

Key Lesson: When you believe in your worth, you command respect and fair compensation.

Action Steps:

- List your skills and accomplishments to reinforce your value.

- Practice self-affirmations such as, "I deserve to be paid what I'm worth."

- Set boundaries to protect your time and expertise.

5. **To Make More, You Have to Invest More:**

Case Study: Elon Musk's relentless investments are a testament to this principle. In 2022, he purchased Twitter for $44 billion, an audacious move that redefined his business portfolio. By 2024, Musk's companies were exploring opportunities in Argentina, continuing to expand his influence and financial growth.

Key Lesson: High returns often demand bold investments. Fear of putting in significant resources' limits growth.

Action Steps:

- Identify areas where strategic investments can amplify returns (e.g., skills, business opportunities, or technology).

- Allocate a portion of your income for calculated, growth-focused investments.

- Overcome fear by researching and educating yourself about potential risks and rewards.

6. **Accept That Loss Is a Reality:**

Case Study: Jeff Bezos often discusses Amazon's failures and emphasizes that losses are necessary for innovation. For instance, Amazon's Fire Phone was a flop, but it paved the way for future successes like Alexa and Echo.

Key Lesson: Losses are stepping stones to growth when approached with the right mindset.

Action Steps:

- Reframe losses as learning opportunities.

- Conduct post-mortem analyses to identify areas for improvement.

- Stay persistent and focus on long-term goals despite setbacks.

7. **Shift from "Making a Living" to "Building Wealth":**

Case Study: Warren Buffett began investing at age 11, focusing on long-term wealth-building strategies rather than immediate gains. His approach turned him into one of the world's richest individuals.

Key Lesson: Wealth-building requires vision and a focus on long-term growth.

Action Steps:

- Educate yourself about investments and financial planning.

- Create a financial roadmap with goals for passive income and asset growth.

- Reinvest profits to compound your wealth.

8. **Develop Courage and Compassion to Say No:**

Case Study: Oprah Winfrey, despite her generous spirit, learned to set boundaries early in her career. By saying no to projects or people that didn't align with her goals, she preserved her energy and time for opportunities that truly mattered.

Key Lesson: Saying no can protect your time, energy, and resources, allowing you to focus on your priorities.

Action Steps:

- Practice saying no with kindness and clarity. For example, "I'd love to help, but I need to focus on my commitments right now."

- Reflect on where you've overcommitted and identify areas to set boundaries.

- Remember: Saying no to others can mean saying yes to your success.

9. **Replace "Risk-Avoidance" with Strategic Risk-Taking:**

Case Study: J.K. Rowling's decision to pursue publishing "Harry Potter" was a calculated risk. Despite initial rejections, her persistence turned the series into a global phenomenon.

Key Lesson: Strategic risks are often the gateway to groundbreaking success.

Action Steps:

- Assess risks by weighing potential rewards against possible losses.

- Start small with low-risk opportunities to build confidence.

- Trust that failure is part of the learning process.

10. **You Have to Be Willing to Lose to Make a Profit:**

Case Study: Richard Branson's Virgin brand expanded into the airline industry despite the high risk of financial loss. Branson's willingness to take bold steps allowed Virgin Atlantic to thrive, despite initial challenges.

Key Lesson: Risking short-term losses is often necessary for long-term gains.

Action Steps:

- Identify areas where calculated risks can lead to substantial rewards.

- Develop contingency plans to manage potential losses.

- Shift your focus to long-term profitability rather than immediate gains.

11. Surround Yourself with Wealth-Positive Influences:

Case Study: Richard Branson credits much of his success to surrounding himself with ambitious and innovative people. His network consistently inspires and challenges him.

Key Lesson: Your environment shapes your mindset and potential.

Action Steps:

- Join communities or masterminds focused on financial growth.

- Seek mentors who embody the values and success you aim to achieve.

- Distance yourself from negativity and scarcity-driven thinking.

Conclusion

Building a happy millionaire mindset requires aligning your thoughts, actions, and environment with your goals. This journey begins with embracing imperfection, cultivating gratitude, and developing the courage to take risks. Recognize that setbacks and losses are natural parts of growth and that long-term wealth comes from persistence, strategic decisions, and a commitment to self-worth.

True wealth is a combination of financial success and personal fulfillment. It's about living with purpose, appreciating abundance, and investing in yourself and your future. Surround yourself with positive influences, take bold steps toward your dreams, and trust the process.

Call to Action

Pick three principles from this chapter to implement over the next week. Start small but stay consistent. Focus on embracing opportunities, learning from failures, and celebrating progress. Remember, the mindset of a happy millionaire isn't just about making money—it's about creating a rich and meaningful life. Your journey starts today.

Chapter 6

The Wealth of Now

"Wealth is the ability to fully experience life ." **– Henry David Thoreau**

In a world often obsessed with chasing future goals and replaying past mistakes, the present moment—"the now"—is frequently overlooked. Yet, it is within the now that the seeds of wealth are planted, nurtured, and harvested. Living in the present moment is not just a spiritual ideal; it's a practical strategy for creating lasting wealth, both material and intangible. This chapter will explore how embracing the present can transform your financial life and pave the way for abundance.

The Power of Focus

Living in the now sharpens your focus. When your mind is anchored in the present, you're not distracted by fears of the future or regrets of the past. This clarity allows you to identify opportunities that others might miss. Consider how many brilliant ideas are lost because someone's attention is scattered. By focusing fully on the task at hand, you can execute it with excellence, setting the foundation for financial success.

For instance, take the story of Sarah, an entrepreneur who struggled with constant overthinking. By committing to daily mindfulness exercises, she began to approach her business tasks with clarity. Within months, her productivity soared, leading to a significant increase in her company's revenue. Sarah's success wasn't about luck; it was about focus.

Making Better Financial Decisions

When you're present, your financial decisions become more thoughtful and deliberate. Instead of impulsively spending out of boredom or fear, you can assess your true needs and align your spending with your values. Mindful living fosters financial discipline, a cornerstone of wealth creation.

Imagine sitting down to evaluate an investment opportunity. If your thoughts are elsewhere, you might overlook crucial details or act out of emotion rather than logic. Conversely, a present-moment mindset enables you to weigh risks and rewards objectively, leading to smarter choices that accumulate wealth over time.

Consider the case of David, who used mindfulness to curb his impulse spending. By pausing before each purchase to ask, "Do I really need this?" he saved thousands of dollars in a year. This newfound financial discipline allowed him to invest in stocks that later doubled in value.

Building Meaningful Connections

Wealth is not only about money; it's also about relationships. Living in the now enhances your ability to connect deeply with others. When you give someone your undivided attention, you build trust and rapport. In the business world, these qualities are invaluable.

Networking is often described as a key to success, but the most powerful networks are built on genuine, present interactions. Whether you're collaborating with a partner, negotiating with a client, or inspiring your team, your presence communicates respect and commitment.

These qualities not only enrich your relationships but also open doors to opportunities that drive financial growth.

For example, Lisa, a marketing consultant, transformed her career by focusing on authentic, present conversations with her clients. Her ability to truly listen not only built trust but also attracted high-profile projects that doubled her income.

Turning Setbacks into Lessons

Life's challenges are inevitable, but how you respond to them shapes your financial future. Living in the now helps you face setbacks with resilience and adaptability. Instead of dwelling on what went wrong, you can focus on what can be done right now to improve the situation.

Consider a failed business venture. A person stuck in the past might wallow in regret, while someone anxious about the future might abandon entrepreneurship altogether. But a present-minded individual evaluates the experience, learns from it, and moves forward with newfound wisdom.

Take the story of Marcus, a tech startup founder whose first venture collapsed. Instead of succumbing to despair, he analyzed his mistakes and implemented changes in his next endeavor. His second company not only succeeded but also became a leader in its industry.

Then there's the case of Priya, a freelance designer who lost her biggest client unexpectedly. Initially devastated, she decided to focus on what she could do immediately. Priya used the time to refine her portfolio and reach out to potential clients. Within weeks, she landed multiple projects, surpassing her previous income.

Another example is James, an aspiring musician who faced repeated rejections from record labels. Instead of giving up or getting lost in self-pity, he concentrated on improving his craft and performing at local venues. His dedication paid off when a viral video of his performance caught the attention of a producer, catapulting his career.

Appreciating Abundance

One of the most overlooked aspects of wealth is gratitude. By living in the now, you become more aware of the abundance already in your life. This mindset shift has a profound impact on your financial behavior. Instead of operating from a place of scarcity, you start to act from a place of sufficiency and possibility.

Gratitude also attracts wealth in subtle ways. When you're genuinely appreciative, you're more likely to nurture what you have—whether it's your skills, investments, or relationships. Over time, this care and attention compound, creating greater abundance.

Practical Action Steps to Embrace the Now

1. **Practice Mindfulness:** Dedicate a few minutes daily to mindfulness exercises, such as meditation or deep breathing. These practices train your mind to stay present.

   - **Start small:** Just five minutes of mindful breathing each morning can make a difference.

2. **Set Intentional Goals:** While it's important to plan for the future, ensure your goals are grounded in actionable steps you can take today.

   - Break long-term goals into daily tasks.

   - Celebrate completing each step to stay motivated.

3. **Eliminate Distractions:** Identify habits or environments that pull you away from the present moment and make changes to stay focused.

   - Create a designated workspace free of clutter.

   - Turn off unnecessary notifications on your devices.

4. **Reflect Daily:** At the end of each day, take a moment to reflect on what you accomplished. Celebrate small wins and identify areas for improvement.

    - Keep a journal to track your progress.

    - Write down three things you're grateful for each night.

5. **Engage Fully:** Whether you're working, spending time with loved ones, or pursuing a hobby, give it your full attention. Presence enhances both enjoyment and effectiveness.

    - Practice active listening in conversations.

    - Avoid multitasking and focus on one thing at a time.

Conclusion

Living in the now is not about ignoring the future or forgetting the past. Instead, it's about grounding yourself in the present as the foundation for all actions. When you harness the power of the now, you unlock clarity, discipline, and creativity—qualities essential for building wealth. Remember, true abundance starts with fully appreciating and leveraging the only moment you ever truly have: this one.

By integrating these practices into your life, you'll not only create financial wealth but also a richer, more fulfilling experience of life itself.

Call to Action

Start living in the wealth of now today! Take a moment to reflect on your current financial actions and mindset. Are you fully present when making decisions, or are distractions pulling you away? Commit to one mindful practice—whether it's pausing before a purchase, practicing gratitude, or setting daily goals—and see how it transforms your relationship with wealth. The power to create abundance begins with your focus and actions in this moment.

Part 3

Relationships and Money

Chapter 7

Communication Strategies to Overcome the Impact of Money in Relationships

*"Marriage is a partnership, and couples can't win with money unless they budget as a team." – **Dave Ramsey***

Money is a sensitive topic in relationships, and its impact can range from mild misunderstandings to significant conflicts. The key to addressing these issues lies in open and effective communication. The dynamics of money and relationships often include cultural, societal, and familial influences, making communication even more critical. This chapter explores practical strategies to navigate these challenges and foster healthier financial discussions, supported by real-life case studies.

The Role of Communication in Financial Harmony

Effective communication serves as the foundation for understanding, trust, and collaboration in relationships. When financial matters are discussed openly, individuals can align their goals, address misunderstandings, and build stronger connections. However, avoiding or mishandling these conversations can lead to resentment, mistrust, and emotional distance.

1. **Establishing a Safe Space for Discussions:**

   Creating a safe and judgment-free environment is essential for productive conversations about money. Both partners or family members should feel comfortable expressing their thoughts without fear of criticism or blame.

   Example:

   Ravi and Meera, a couple from Mumbai, struggled to discuss their finances due to Ravi's tendency to dismiss Meera's concerns as overly cautious. After attending a financial counseling session, they learned to set aside dedicated time to discuss money without interruptions, creating a space where both felt heard.

2. **Practicing Active Listening:**

   Active listening involves genuinely focusing on what the other person is saying, rather than preparing a rebuttal or interrupting. Acknowledge emotions and validate concerns to build trust.

   Case Study:

   Sanjay, a software engineer, frequently argued with his wife, Priyanka, about her habit of saving excessively. By practicing active listening, Sanjay discovered that Priyanka's saving habits stemmed from financial insecurity rooted in her upbringing. Understanding this helped him approach the issue with empathy, leading to constructive solutions.

3. **Using "I" Statements Instead of Blame:**

   Framing concerns with "I" statements helps to express feelings without assigning blame. For example, instead of saying, "You never save enough," say, "I feel anxious about our future when we don't save."

Example:

Rohit and Shalini's arguments often escalated because they accused each other of financial irresponsibility. Shalini started using "I" statements to express her worries, which diffused tensions and encouraged mutual understanding.

4. **Aligning Financial Goals:**

Partners and families should regularly discuss and align their financial goals, such as saving for a home, children's education, or retirement. This ensures everyone works toward shared objectives, reducing conflicts.

Case Study:

The Verma family in Pune had frequent disagreements about spending. After sitting together to create a family budget that included contributions from everyone, they found their collective goals brought them closer and reduced arguments.

5. **Being Transparent and Honest:**

Financial transparency builds trust and eliminates the risk of unpleasant surprises. Discussing debts, expenses, and financial aspirations openly prevents misunderstandings and fosters accountability.

Example:

Aditi, a marketing professional, hid her credit card debt from her husband, Sameer, fearing judgment. When Sameer eventually discovered it, he felt betrayed. They sought financial counseling, where Aditi's honesty helped rebuild trust, and they worked together to clear the debt.

6. **Understanding Emotional Triggers:**

Recognize the emotional underpinnings of financial behaviors. For instance, one partner's spending might stem from a desire for immediate gratification, while the other's saving might be driven by anxiety.

Case Study:

Manish and Kavya often clashed because Manish enjoyed frequent shopping, while Kavya prioritized saving. Through open conversations, Kavya learned that shopping was Manish's way of coping with stress. Together, they found healthier outlets for stress relief and set limits on discretionary spending.

7. **Seeking Professional Guidance:**

When financial conflicts persist, seeking guidance from a financial advisor or counselor can provide an objective perspective. Professionals can mediate discussions, offering tailored solutions.

Example:

The Sharma family in Delhi, overwhelmed by conflicting financial priorities among siblings and parents, sought help from a financial planner. The expert facilitated discussions, helping the family draft a plan that addressed both individual and collective needs.

8. **Setting Boundaries and Expectations:**

Clearly defining financial boundaries—such as limits on lending money to extended family or agreeing on monthly discretionary spending—can prevent future conflicts.

Case Study:

Deepak and Nisha, a couple from Chennai, often argued about lending money to relatives. They agreed to set a monthly limit on such expenses, ensuring they supported the family without compromising their financial security.

Conclusion

Open and empathetic communication is a powerful tool for addressing the impact of money on relationships. By establishing safe spaces, practicing active listening, aligning goals, and seeking professional guidance when needed, individuals can navigate financial challenges with confidence and mutual respect.

Call to Action

Understanding the psychological impact of money on relationships is only the beginning. Applying these communication strategies can transform how you and your loved ones navigate financial matters. In the next chapter, we will delve into actionable steps for building a robust financial foundation that supports healthy relationships and long-term well-being. Stay tuned!

Chapter 8

Collaborative Financial Decision-Making to Strengthen Relationships

*"The goal in marriage is not to think alike about money, but to think together." – **Robert C. Dodds***

Collaborative financial decision-making is not just about managing money; it is about fostering trust, understanding, and partnership in relationships. For Indian families and couples, financial collaboration is deeply influenced by cultural norms, societal expectations, and the unique dynamics of joint families. When approached thoughtfully, shared financial decisions can strengthen bonds, align goals, and create a sense of unity.

This chapter explores how collaborative financial decision-making can transform relationships, supported by real-life case studies, and concludes with actionable insights.

The Importance of Collaborative Financial Decisions

In a relationship, financial collaboration ensures that both parties feel valued and involved. This approach minimizes misunderstandings, prevents power imbalances, and helps in achieving shared goals. In India, where family obligations and societal pressures are significant, working together on financial matters becomes even more crucial.

1. **Shared Responsibility and Accountability:**

    When financial decisions are made collaboratively, each member takes responsibility for the outcomes. This shared accountability reduces the risk of blame-shifting during financial setbacks and fosters a sense of teamwork.

    In collaborative arrangements, everyone's contribution—whether financial or non-financial—is acknowledged. This could mean discussing how household chores, caregiving, or other forms of labor indirectly impact financial health.

    Case Study:

    Arjun and Kavita, a couple from Hyderabad, initially struggled with managing household expenses. Arjun handled all financial decisions, which left Kavita feeling excluded and undervalued. After attending a financial planning workshop, they decided to create monthly budgets together. By sharing responsibilities, they not only improved their financial stability but also built a stronger emotional connection as equal partners.

2. **Building Trust Through Transparency:**

    Transparency is the bedrock of trust in financial collaboration. It involves open discussions about income, expenses, debts, savings, and investments. When both parties are aware of each other's financial standing, it eliminates the potential for suspicion or conflict.

    Financial secrecy, on the other hand, can erode trust and lead to misunderstandings. Transparency also ensures that everyone has access to the same information, enabling more informed and balanced decisions.

Example:

The Gupta family in Jaipur faced challenges when Ramesh, the primary earner, kept his investments private. His wife, Sunita, felt mistrusted and uninvolved. When Ramesh finally shared all financial details during a family discussion, Sunita's confidence in their partnership was restored. This openness also encouraged her to contribute ideas for improving their investments, resulting in a more collaborative approach.

3. **Aligning Financial Goals:**

Collaborative decision-making allows couples and families to align their financial goals. These goals could range from short-term objectives, like reducing monthly expenses, to long-term aspirations, such as buying property, funding children's education, or planning for retirement.

Aligning financial goals requires understanding each other's priorities, values, and aspirations. Differences in priorities are natural, but they can be reconciled through open communication and compromise.

Case Study:

Vikram and Neha, a newlywed couple from Bengaluru, had conflicting financial priorities. Vikram wanted to invest in a new car, while Neha emphasized saving for a down payment on a house. By consulting a financial advisor together, they learned to balance both goals by delaying the car purchase and allocating savings strategically. This approach not only resolved their conflict but also strengthened their partnership through mutual respect and compromise.

4. **Cultural and Familial Considerations:**

In India, financial decisions often extend beyond nuclear families to include extended relatives. Joint families may pool resources, and individuals may face expectations to contribute to family events, support parents, or assist siblings. Collaborative decision-making helps address these obligations without compromising individual or nuclear family needs.

Example:

The Sharma family in Kolkata faced a dilemma when planning their son's wedding. Pooling resources ensured that the financial burden was distributed among family members. By involving everyone in budgeting and planning, they ensured transparency and avoided conflicts. The collective effort also strengthened family bonds, allowing them to honor traditions without financial strain.

5. **Strengthening Emotional Bonds:**

   Collaborating on financial matters goes beyond practical benefits; it strengthens emotional connections by fostering communication, understanding, and a shared sense of purpose. Working together on budgets, savings, or investments allows partners and family members to feel united in achieving common objectives.

   Case Study:

   Ananya and Rohit, parents of two from Pune, involved their teenage children in discussions about household expenses and savings. This not only taught their children the value of financial planning but also created a sense of teamwork within the family. The collaborative approach made everyone feel responsible and valued, enhancing their overall family dynamic.

Steps for Effective Financial Collaboration

Step 1: Set Clear Goals:

Begin by identifying and prioritizing shared financial goals. Discuss both individual and collective aspirations, such as saving for a family vacation, reducing debt, or investing in property. Ensure that these goals reflect the input and priorities of all involved parties.

Step 2: Create a Joint Budget:

Develop a budget that outlines income, expenses, and savings contributions from everyone. This ensures transparency, accountability, and a clear understanding of where resources are allocated. A joint budget also helps in setting realistic expectations.

Step 3: Leverage Technology:

Use financial planning apps and tools to track expenses, set reminders, and monitor progress toward goals. These tools can simplify data sharing and make the process more efficient.

Step 4: Schedule Regular Check-ins:

Set aside dedicated time to review financial plans, discuss changes, and address concerns. Regular check-ins ensure that everyone remains aligned with the agreed-upon objectives and can adapt to new circumstances or challenges.

Step 5: Seek Professional Advice:

Engage a financial advisor or mediator when decisions are particularly complex or contentious. Professionals can provide unbiased perspectives and help create actionable plans that accommodate all viewpoints.

Step 6: Acknowledge Contributions:

Recognize and value everyone's contributions, whether financial or non-financial. This acknowledgment fosters inclusivity and ensures that all parties feel appreciated for their role in achieving shared goals.

Conclusion

Collaborative financial decision-making is a cornerstone of strong relationships. By sharing responsibilities, maintaining transparency, and aligning goals, families and couples can navigate financial challenges with unity and resilience. In India, where cultural and familial obligations often shape financial decisions, collaboration ensures that everyone's needs and aspirations are addressed.

Call to Action

Take a moment to evaluate the level of collaboration in your financial decision-making. Are all voices being heard and valued? Start by initiating an open conversation about financial goals, responsibilities, and transparency with your partner or family. Use the steps outlined in this chapter—such as setting shared goals, creating a joint budget, or scheduling regular check-ins—to strengthen trust, unity, and understanding in your relationships. Begin today and see the difference it can make in fostering stronger connections and a more resilient financial future.

Part 4

Practical Financial Tools

Chapter 9

Becoming Wealthy vs. Staying Wealthy

"Diversification may preserve wealth, but concentration builds wealth"
- Warren Buffet

Introduction

Wealth creation and wealth preservation are two sides of the same coin, yet they require entirely different mindsets and strategies. While becoming wealthy often demands risk-taking, innovation, and hard work, staying wealthy hinges on prudence, discipline, and adaptability. Understanding the nuances of this balance is essential, given the rapid economic changes and cultural expectations surrounding wealth.

The Journey of Becoming Wealthy

Becoming wealthy involves a combination of factors such as ambition, strategic decision-making, and perseverance. Key elements include:

1. **Taking Calculated Risks**: Wealth creation often requires venturing into uncharted territory—be it starting a business, investing in emerging markets, or pursuing higher education abroad. Calculated risks differ from reckless gambles by being

informed and measured, ensuring that potential losses are manageable.

2. **Leveraging Opportunities**: Successful wealth creators are adept at identifying and capitalizing on opportunities, whether in technology, real estate, or equity markets. For example, investing in emerging industries or leveraging government policies designed to encourage entrepreneurship can provide significant returns.

3. **Consistent Hard Work**: Most self-made wealthy individuals attribute their success to years of focused effort and persistence. Staying consistent, even during periods of uncertainty or setbacks, is a hallmark of successful wealth creators.

4. **Financial Literacy**: Understanding investments, taxation, and business operations plays a crucial role in building wealth. The ability to read financial statements, interpret market trends, and assess risks ensures informed decision-making.

5. **Networking and Mentorship**: Surrounding oneself with like-minded, ambitious individuals and seeking mentorship from experienced professionals can accelerate the path to wealth. Connections often lead to opportunities that might otherwise remain inaccessible.

Case Study 1: Ramesh's Entrepreneurial Success

Ramesh, a first-generation entrepreneur from Chennai, started a small IT services company with a loan and limited resources. Through dedication and a knack for identifying client needs, he grew his business into a multimillion-dollar enterprise over a decade. Ramesh's willingness to take calculated risks and reinvest profits was instrumental in his wealth creation journey. However, his story also highlights the importance of learning from mistakes; an initial expansion failure taught him the value of market research and planning.

Case Study 2: Meera's Investment Acumen

Meera, a software engineer in Bengaluru, began investing 20% of her salary in equity mutual funds and stocks at the age of 25. Her disciplined approach, combined with a focus on high-growth industries like renewable energy and technology, allowed her portfolio to grow significantly over a decade. Meera's success was rooted in her commitment to continuous learning and her decision to seek professional advice during volatile markets.

The Challenge of Staying Wealthy

While becoming wealthy is challenging, staying wealthy can be even more difficult. Factors that threaten long-term wealth include:

1. **Lifestyle Inflation**: As income grows, so do expenses. Many individuals succumb to upgrading their lifestyles, often at the expense of savings and investments. This phenomenon is particularly visible in India, where societal pressures to showcase wealth through lavish weddings, luxury cars, or upscale homes can erode financial stability.

2. **Overconfidence**: Wealth creators sometimes overestimate their ability to sustain success, leading to risky investments or business decisions. This overconfidence can manifest as a disregard for diversification or excessive reliance on speculative ventures.

3. **Economic Downturns**: Recessions, market crashes, and unexpected financial crises can erode wealth rapidly. Without a robust financial plan, even substantial fortunes can dwindle during prolonged downturns.

4. **Lack of Diversification**: Over-reliance on a single source of income or asset class increases vulnerability. For instance, a businessperson who invests solely in their industry risks significant losses if market dynamics shift.

5. **Poor Succession Planning**: Inadequate planning for wealth transfer often leads to disputes and financial instability within families. A lack of clear wills, trusts, or succession frameworks can result in legal battles and a dilution of wealth.

6. **Inflation and Taxation**: Without proper investment strategies, wealth can diminish in real terms due to inflation and high taxation. Keeping funds in low-yield assets or failing to optimize tax liabilities can significantly impact long-term financial stability.

Case Study 3: The Missteps of the Gupta Family

The Gupta family from Delhi inherited significant wealth from their textile business. However, excessive spending, lack of diversification, and internal family conflicts led to a rapid depletion of their fortune within two generations. This highlights the importance of careful financial planning, effective communication within families, and disciplined investment strategies in preserving wealth.

Case Study 4: The Sharma Legacy

The Sharma's, a business family from Pune, built a successful pharmaceutical company over three decades. Recognizing the importance of staying wealthy, they set up a family office to manage their investments and implemented a succession plan that included clear roles for the next generation. They also diversified into real estate and international markets, ensuring that their wealth remained resilient despite fluctuations in the pharmaceutical sector.

Strategies to Stay Wealthy

To sustain wealth, individuals and families must adopt disciplined and proactive measures:

1. **Diversify Investments**: Spread investments across asset classes like equities, bonds, real estate, and gold to reduce risk. Diversification ensures that losses in one area can be offset by gains in another.

2. **Adopt a Conservative Approach**: Once wealth is created, prioritize preservation over aggressive growth. This might mean shifting to more stable investments, such as government bonds or blue-chip stocks.

3. **Focus on Financial Planning**: Regularly review financial goals and ensure adequate insurance coverage. Planning for unexpected events, such as medical emergencies or market crashes, is crucial.

4. **Live Below Your Means**: Resist the temptation to inflate your lifestyle unnecessarily. Instead, focus on long-term financial stability. Simple practices like budgeting and tracking expenses can make a significant difference.

5. **Educate the Next Generation**: Teach children the value of money, investing, and responsibility to ensure continuity in wealth management. Instilling financial literacy early on helps prevent reckless spending and mismanagement.

6. **Engage Professionals**: Work with financial advisors, tax consultants, and estate planners to make informed decisions. Professionals can provide valuable insights into market trends, tax-saving strategies, and asset protection.

7. **Establish a Contingency Fund**: Maintain a fund to address unexpected expenses or economic downturns, ensuring that long-term investments remain untouched during crises.

Case Study 5: The Resilience of the Shah Family

The Shah family from Mumbai built their wealth through a thriving export business. To safeguard their fortune, they diversified into mutual funds, real estate, and blue-chip stocks. They also established a family office to manage their wealth professionally and educated their children in finance and governance. This foresight ensured their wealth remained intact across generations.

Case Study 6: The Power of an Emergency Fund

Vikram, a senior executive in Kolkata, faced an unexpected job loss during the COVID-19 pandemic. His six-month emergency fund allowed him to sustain his family's lifestyle and avoid dipping into long-term investments. Vikram's foresight in maintaining a contingency fund reinforced his financial stability.

Conclusion

The journey of wealth creation and preservation requires distinct skill sets and mindsets. While becoming wealthy demands vision, hard work, and risk-taking, staying wealthy calls for prudence, discipline, and adaptability. For Indian families, cultural values, societal expectations, and economic changes add unique dimensions to this challenge. By balancing these dynamics, individuals and families can ensure that their wealth not only grows but also endures.

Call to Action

Whether you are on the path to becoming wealthy or striving to preserve your fortune, remember that financial success is a marathon, not a sprint. Start by educating yourself and your family, diversifying investments, and seeking professional advice. Most importantly, stay humble and disciplined—true wealth is not just about accumulating money but also sustaining it over time. Act today to secure a prosperous future for yourself and the generations to come.

Chapter 10

The True Cost of Homeownership – A Decision That Shapes Your Financial Future

*"Risk comes from not knowing what you're doing." – **Warren Buffett***

Buying a house is one of the most significant financial decisions in a person's life. It is not just about owning a property but about securing long-term financial stability and ensuring peace of mind. A well-timed and well-planned purchase can provide security, while an impulsive or poorly calculated decision can disrupt personal finances and strain family relationships. This chapter explores the key factors that determine the right time to buy a house, the impact of a wrong decision, and real-life examples to illustrate how financial discipline in this regard leads to a stable and fulfilling life.

The Financial Impact of Buying a House

Purchasing a home involves a substantial financial commitment, including a down payment, monthly EMIs, maintenance costs, property taxes, and unexpected expenses like repairs or renovations. A well-planned purchase ensures affordability without sacrificing other financial goals, whereas a poorly considered purchase can lead to debt traps, stress, and financial instability.

A wrong decision in home buying can have extreme consequences, especially if unforeseen circumstances arise:

Example 1: Rohan, a marketing professional in Bangalore, took a massive home loan, confident that his rising salary would cover the EMI. However, a sudden industry downturn resulted in him losing his job. With no emergency fund and a heavy EMI burden, he defaulted on his home loan, forcing him to sell his house at a loss. This financial setback delayed his career recovery and forced him to make lifestyle compromises.

Example 2: Neha and her husband bought a house in Mumbai by stretching their finances to the limit. A few years later, an unexpected medical emergency required costly treatments. Since their savings were tied up in EMI payments, they had to take high-interest loans, pushing them into a debt spiral. What should have been their dream home turned into a financial nightmare, causing stress and conflicts within the family.

Example 3: Suresh, a self-employed entrepreneur, purchased a high-value home assuming his business income would continue growing. When the market slowed down, his revenue dropped significantly, and he struggled to pay his EMI. Without a diversified investment portfolio or emergency funds, he had to liquidate personal assets at a loss, causing severe financial instability.

These cases highlight the importance of planning for contingencies and ensuring that homeownership does not lead to financial instability.

Key Factors to Consider Before Buying a House

1. Financial Readiness:

Before committing to a home purchase, ensure that:

You have a stable income source.

You have an emergency fund covering at least 6-12 months of expenses.

Your existing debt is under control (preferably less than 40% of your monthly income).

You can make a minimum down payment of 20% of the house price.

Example: Ananya, working in Bangalore, waited until she saved ₹20 lakhs for a down payment. She bought a house that required an EMI of only 30% of her monthly income, allowing her to continue saving and investing for her future. This strategic approach helped her build a diversified investment portfolio, giving her financial freedom at an early stage.

Example: Vijay, an engineer in Mumbai, initially planned to buy a house but realized that his savings were insufficient. Instead of rushing, he spent two years increasing his emergency fund and clearing other debts. When he finally purchased his home, he was financially secure and stress-free.

2. EMI Affordability Based on Income:

A practical rule is that your home loan EMI should not exceed 30-40% of your monthly income. Here's an example breakdown:

Monthly Income (₹)	Suggested EMI (₹)
50,000	15,000 (30%)
1,00,000	30,000 (30%)
1,50,000	45,000 (30%)

Example: Pranav, earning ₹1,00,000 in Mumbai, was initially tempted to buy a ₹2 crore home. However, he wisely chose a ₹90 lakh property instead, keeping his EMI within 30% of his income. This decision allowed him to maintain his lifestyle without financial stress and continue investing in mutual funds and stocks. Over 15 years, his disciplined approach helped him build a corpus of ₹3.5 crores, which covered his children's education, regular vacations, and quality medical care. Now financially independent, Pranav can retire early and pursue his passion for traveling.

Example: Meenal, a doctor, bought a house with an EMI of ₹50,000 while earning ₹2,00,000 per month. Because her EMI was only 25% of her income, she was able to consistently invest and build a retirement fund without financial stress.

Good Decisions in Home Buying – Financially Secure Homeowners

While some people struggle due to poor financial planning, others make wise decisions that lead to financial stability and a comfortable lifestyle. Here are three examples of individuals who followed sound financial principles when buying their homes and how it helped them achieve financial security.

Example 1: Rajiv and Meera, a couple in Bangalore, bought a ₹1.2 crore apartment by making a 30% down payment (₹36 lakhs) and keeping their EMI at 25% of their combined monthly income of ₹2.5 lakhs. Because they kept their EMI low, they continued investing ₹50,000 per month in equity mutual funds. After 12 years, their investments had grown to ₹2.5 crores, ensuring their children's education was fully funded while they still enjoyed vacations and a comfortable life.

Example 2: Anil, a senior software engineer in Mumbai, resisted the urge to buy a sea-facing luxury apartment and instead purchased a ₹1.5 crore flat in an emerging suburb. He ensured his EMI was only 30% of his ₹3 lakh monthly salary and invested the remaining ₹70,000 in a diversified portfolio. Over 15 years, his investments grew to ₹4 crores, allowing him to retire early and pursue his passion for teaching technology to underprivileged children.

Example 3: Pooja, a single working professional in Pune, planned her home purchase meticulously. She saved for 8 years and made a 40% down payment on a ₹90 lakh apartment, keeping her EMI at just 20%

of her monthly salary of ₹1.5 lakhs. With financial discipline, she built a retirement corpus of ₹3 crores alongside owning a fully paid home, allowing her to quit her corporate job at 50 and transition into a relaxed freelance career.

These examples highlight how following personal finance principles—like maintaining a reasonable EMI, making a higher down payment, and continuing investments—can lead to financial freedom and stress-free homeownership.

When Renting is a Better Option?

In metro cities like Mumbai and Bangalore, renting can often be a smarter financial choice due to high property prices and lower rental yields. Renting allows individuals to maintain financial flexibility, invest in higher-return assets, and avoid the financial strain of large EMIs.

When does renting make more sense?

- If home prices are significantly high compared to monthly rent.

- If your job requires frequent relocation.

- If you can invest the money you save on EMIs in high-return assets.

Example 1: Priya was considering buying a 2BHK apartment in Mumbai for ₹1.5 crores with an EMI of ₹1 lakh per month. Instead, she chose to rent a similar apartment for ₹40,000 per month and invested the remaining ₹60,000 in mutual funds. Over 15 years, her corpus grew to ₹4 crores, giving her financial freedom. She could now buy a home without any loan if she wished, or continue living stress-free while pursuing her interests.

Example 2: Amit, an IT consultant in Bangalore, rents a luxurious apartment for ₹50,000 instead of buying a ₹2 crore property. He invests his savings aggressively and has built a solid portfolio, giving him the flexibility to relocate or retire early. Over 12 years, his investments compounded to ₹3.2 crores, allowing him to retire at 45 and pursue travel and writing.

Example 3: Rakesh and Nidhi, a working couple in Mumbai, chose to rent instead of buying a ₹3 crore house. Instead, they continued investing ₹1 lakh per month into equity and real estate funds. After 18 years, their investment portfolio grew to ₹6.5 crores, securing their children's education abroad and giving them an early retirement option without any financial burden.

These examples show how renting, combined with disciplined investments, can provide financial security and lifestyle flexibility.

Living Holistically Beyond Homeownership

A house is just one aspect of financial well-being, and prioritizing it over everything else can lead to unnecessary compromises in life. True financial success means living a well-rounded life, which includes:

Enjoying meaningful experiences such as travel and family time.

Maintaining good health without worrying about financial burdens.

Investing in personal and professional growth opportunities.

Building relationships and spending time with loved ones without financial stress.

Example 1: Rahul focused on holistic financial well-being rather than rushing into homeownership. By renting and investing wisely, he was able to take frequent vacations, fund his children's education without stress, and retire early to pursue his dream of starting a non-profit organization.

Example 2: Kavita and Arjun decided to buy a modest home instead of a luxury apartment. This decision allowed them to save for their children's education, take international vacations, and maintain a stress-free financial life. They prioritized experiences and financial security over the pressure of owning an expensive home.

Example 3: Nikhil chose to stay on rent while pursuing his dream of starting a business. By avoiding the financial burden of a home loan, he was able to invest in his business and grow it successfully. A few years later, he had both a profitable business and enough savings to buy a house without stress.

Conclusion: Making the Right Decision

A home purchase should be a well-calculated decision rather than an emotional impulse. Buying a house too soon or without proper financial preparation can lead to financial distress, whereas a planned purchase results in stability and prosperity.

Action Steps to Take Before Buying a Home

1. **Assess Your Financial Health:** Ensure you have a stable income, minimal debts, and an emergency fund that covers at least 6-12 months of expenses.

2. **Calculate Affordability:** Ensure your EMI does not exceed 30-40% of your monthly income, and factor in all additional costs like maintenance, property tax, and home insurance.

3. **Research the Market:** Check home price trends, loan interest rates, and property appreciation potential before making a decision.

4. **Compare Renting vs. Buying:** If renting allows you to invest and grow wealth without financial strain, consider it as a better option before rushing into homeownership.

5. **Plan for Long-Term Stability:** Consider job security, family growth, and possible relocations before making a commitment.

6. **Think Holistically:** Ensure that your home purchase does not come at the cost of other life goals, such as travel, children's education, or financial independence.

Call to Action

Homeownership is a significant milestone, but it should not come at the cost of financial stress and lost opportunities. Evaluate your financial situation, consider all aspects of the decision, and make a choice that aligns with your long-term goals. If renting offers greater financial security and flexibility, do not hesitate to embrace it. Smart decisions today will lead to a secure and fulfilling future!

Chapter 11

Managing Debt and Avoiding Debt Traps

"Debt is like any other trap, easy enough to get into,
*but hard enough to get out of." – **Henry Wheeler Shaw***

Debt is a reality for many, yet with proper management, it need not be a burden. For the common person, debt often stems from necessities like education, healthcare, or unforeseen emergencies. This chapter explores practical strategies to manage and repay debt faster, with real-life case studies. We'll also discuss ways to avoid falling into debt traps and conclude with actionable steps to achieve financial freedom.

Section 1: Understanding Debt Management

Debt management involves planning and executing strategies to handle debt responsibly. The goal is to ensure timely repayments while maintaining financial stability.

Key Principles of Debt Management:

1. **Assess Your Debt:** List all debts, including the amount, interest rate, and repayment terms.

2. **Prioritize Payments:** Focus on high-interest debts first while maintaining minimum payments on others.

3. **Budgeting:** Create a realistic budget to allocate funds towards debt repayment.

4. **Avoid Additional Debt:** Resist the urge to borrow further unless absolutely necessary.

5. **Seek Professional Advice:** Consult financial advisors for structured debt repayment plans if needed.

Section 2: Strategies to Repay Debt Faster

1. **The Debt Snowball Method:**

   - Focus on repaying the smallest debt first while making minimum payments on others.

   - Provides psychological motivation as small debts get cleared quickly.

2. **The Debt Avalanche Method:**

   - Prioritize high-interest debts first to minimize overall interest costs.

   - Requires discipline but is more cost-effective in the long term.

3. **Debt Consolidation:**

   - Combine multiple debts into a single loan with a lower interest rate.

   - Simplifies repayment and can reduce the financial burden.

4. **Increase Income Sources:**

   - Take up part-time work or freelancing to generate additional income for debt repayment.

5. **Negotiate with Creditors:**

    -   Discuss the possibility of lower interest rates or extended repayment terms.

Section 3: Case Studies

Case Study 1: Rajesh, the IT Professional:

Rajesh, a 30-year-old software engineer from Bengaluru, had accumulated credit card debt of ₹200,000. The high interest was eating into his savings. He opted for the **Debt Avalanche Method**, focusing on his highest-interest card first. He also cut down discretionary expenses like dining out and used the savings to make extra payments. Within 18 months, Rajesh was debt-free and had built an emergency fund to avoid future debt.

Case Study 2: Priya, the Small Business Owner:

Priya, a 40-year-old entrepreneur from Pune, had taken multiple loans for her handicrafts business. The EMIs became unmanageable during a downturn. She consolidated her loans into a single business loan with a lower interest rate. Additionally, Priya negotiated better payment terms with her suppliers. By adopting a strict budget and increasing online sales, she cleared her debts in three years.

Section 4: Avoiding Debt Traps

1. **Live Within Your Means:** Avoid unnecessary expenses and luxury purchases.

2. **Emergency Fund:** Maintain a fund covering 3-6 months of expenses for unforeseen situations.

3. **Limit Credit Card Usage:** Use credit cards judiciously and pay the full amount monthly.

4. **Understand Loan Terms:** Read the fine print to ensure transparency in interest rates and penalties.

5. **Financial Education:** Equip yourself with basic financial knowledge to make informed decisions.

Case Study 3: Anjali, the Young Professional:

Anjali, a 25-year-old marketing executive in Mumbai, fell into a debt trap due to impulsive shopping and relying on multiple credit cards. After missing payments, her credit score plummeted. She sought financial counseling and switched to using a debit card for daily expenses. Anjali also started saving 20% of her salary each month. Over time, she repaid her debts and regained financial stability.

Case Study 4: Suresh, the Family Man:

Suresh, a 45-year-old government employee from Chennai, struggled with multiple personal loans taken for his children's education and family emergencies. To avoid a deeper debt trap, he reorganized his finances by cutting down on non-essential expenses and using a portion of his annual bonus for repayments. Suresh also started carpooling to reduce transportation costs. With consistent effort and better planning, he cleared his debts within five years and began investing for future financial security.

Conclusion

Managing and repaying debt requires discipline, planning, and informed decision-making. By adopting strategies like the Debt Avalanche or Snowball Methods, consolidating loans, and living within one's means, financial freedom is achievable. The key is to act early and stay committed to the plan.

Action Steps

1. List all debts and prioritize repayments.

2. Create a monthly budget to track income and expenses.

3. Choose a debt repayment strategy (snowball or avalanche).

4. Explore additional income sources to accelerate repayment.

5. Build an emergency fund to prevent future debt.

Call to Action

Take control of your finances today. Start by assessing your debt and committing to a repayment plan. Seek professional advice if necessary and empower yourself with financial literacy. Remember, every small step brings you closer to a debt-free future.

Chapter 12

Compound Interest – The Eighth Wonder of the World

*"Compound interest is proof that you can get rich slowly." – **Dave Ramsey***

Albert Einstein famously described compound interest as the "eighth wonder of the world." It's a financial principle that has the power to grow wealth exponentially over time. For the common person, understanding and leveraging compound interest can be a life-changing revelation. This chapter delves into the concept of compound interest, explores various investment modes, and provides relatable case studies to illustrate its transformative potential.

What is compound interest?

Compound interest is the process of earning interest on both the initial principal and the previously earned interest. Unlike simple interest, which only applies to the principal amount, compound interest accelerates wealth growth by reinvesting earned interest back into the principal.

Formula:

$$A = P\left(1 + \frac{r}{n}\right)^{nt}$$

Where:

- **A** = Future Value

- **P** = Principal Amount

- **r** = Annual Interest Rate (in decimal form)

- **n** = Number of Compounding Periods per Year

- **t** = Time (in years)

Section 2: Investment Modes for Compounding

1. **Fixed Deposits (FDs):**

   - Offered by banks and post offices with periodic compounding.

   - Suitable for risk-averse investors.

2. **Public Provident Fund (PPF):**

   - A government-backed, tax-free savings scheme with annual compounding.

   - A lock-in period of 15 years encourages long-term growth.

3. **Mutual Funds:**

   - Equity mutual funds and SIPs (Systematic Investment Plans) leverage market growth for higher compounding returns.

   - Higher risk but potential for significant long-term gains.

4. **National Savings Certificate (NSC):**

   - A low-risk investment option with compounded interest.

   - Offered by the government via post offices.

5. **Recurring Deposits (RDs):**

   - Allows periodic savings with compounded interest.

   - Ideal for disciplined, small-scale savers.

6. **Stock Market Investments:**

   - Long-term investments in blue-chip stocks benefit from both dividends and capital appreciation.

   - Requires a good understanding of market trends.

Section 3: Case Studies

Case Study 1: Nitin, the IT Professional:

Nitin, a 28-year-old software engineer from Hyderabad, started investing ₹10,000 per month in a mutual fund SIP. Assuming an average annual return of 12%, his investment grew to ₹1.5 crore over 20 years. By starting early, Nitin leveraged the power of compounding to secure a comfortable retirement.

Case Study 2: Meera, the Homemaker:

Meera, a 35-year-old homemaker from Kochi, invested ₹200,000 in a PPF account with an annual compounding rate of 7.1%. Over 15 years, her investment grew to ₹4,06,000. She used this amount to fund her daughter's higher education, demonstrating how disciplined, risk-free investments can meet future goals.

Case Study 3: Ramesh, the Businessman:

Ramesh, a 45-year-old entrepreneur from Jaipur, diversified his savings between fixed deposits and equity mutual funds. His FD compounded at 6% annually, while his equity mutual fund provided 14% returns over 10 years. By balancing risk and security, Ramesh built a corpus of ₹5,000,000 for his retirement.

Case Study 4: Kavita, the Young Professional:

Kavita, a 22-year-old graphic designer from Bengaluru, started investing in stocks with a modest sum of ₹50,000. By reinvesting dividends and capital gains, her portfolio grew at an average annual rate of 15%. Within 10 years, her wealth quadrupled, allowing her to buy her dream home.

Section 4: Key Takeaways on Compound Interest

1. **Start Early:** The earlier you invest, the more time your money has to grow.

2. **Consistency Matters:** Regular contributions amplify the compounding effect.

3. **Diversify Investments:** Spread your portfolio across multiple modes to balance risk and reward.

4. **Reinvest Returns:** Avoid withdrawing earnings to maximize growth.

5. **Leverage Tax Benefits:** Use tax-saving instruments like PPF and ELSS (Equity Linked Savings Scheme).

Conclusion

Compound interest isn't just a financial concept—it's a wealth-building force that rewards patience and discipline. Whether you're just starting or refining your investment strategy, the key is to stay committed. Time is your greatest ally, and every rupee invested today has the potential to multiply in ways you never imagined. Harness this power, and you can turn your financial aspirations into reality.

Action Steps

1. Identify your financial goals and risk tolerance.

2. Open investment accounts suitable for compounding (e.g., PPF, SIPs, FDs).

3. Start investing a fixed amount regularly, no matter how small.

4. Monitor your investments periodically and adjust as needed.

5. Stay disciplined and avoid premature withdrawals.

Call to Action

The longer you wait, the more opportunities you miss. Start now—choose an investment, commit to consistent contributions, and let compounding do the rest. Your future self will thank you for the decision you make today.

Chapter 13

Understanding and Achieving Ultimate Financial Freedom

"The goal isn't more money. The goal is living life on your terms."
– Chris Brogan

Imagine waking up every day without financial worries, just like Ankit. At 42, Ankit feels relaxed and peaceful because his financial freedom allows him to plan long-awaited trips and enjoy life to the fullest. This peace is within your reach too. Financial freedom is not just a dream—it's a goal you can achieve with clarity, focus, and action.

The Power of Financial Freedom

Financial freedom brings immense benefits:

1. **Reduced Stress:** No more paycheck-to-paycheck living or debt burdens.

2. **Flexibility:** Freedom to spend time and money pursuing your passions.

3. **Peace of Mind:** A financial cushion for life's unexpected challenges.

4. **Control:** Making empowered financial choices.

5. **Freedom to Dream:** Aligning your goals with your values and interests.

Ankit achieved his financial freedom by understanding two critical concepts: DCLE (Daily Comfortable Living Expenses) and FDG (Financial Desire Goals). Let's explore these in detail.

Understanding DCLE and FDG

DCLE represents the amount required for a comfortable daily lifestyle. It covers not just the essentials, but also the experiences that make life more enjoyable — such as:

- Weekly family dinners at your favorite restaurant.
- Movies twice a month.
- Quarterly holidays.
- Thoughtful Diwali gifts for loved ones.
- Renting a spacious, comfortable home

Example

Suppose your monthly rent is ₹25,000 and your regular household expenses come to ₹30,000. In addition, you spend around ₹15,000 each month on weekly family dinners, movie outings, and quarterly vacations. In this case, your total monthly DCLE would be ₹70,000.

In contrast, FDG involves aspirations that may tie you to financial stress, such as:

- Buying a 4BHK in the most expensive area of the city.
- Annual international holidays only.
- Driving a luxury car instead of any reliable vehicle.

The Trap of Financial Desire Goals

Many confuse FDG with financial freedom, unknowingly becoming slaves to their desires. Take the story of Ankur and Mohini, who earn a handsome ₹5 lakhs monthly but feel stressed and trapped. With two houses, two cars, and dreams of expensive schooling for their baby, they barely enjoy life. Their focus on FDGs led to this financial strain.

When they shifted their focus to DCLE and recalculated their needs, they made bold changes: selling one house, reducing their expenses, and investing wisely. Now, they live peacefully, with time for their child and clarity in their goals.

The Path to Financial Freedom: Ankit's Story

Ankit's journey to financial freedom began seven years ago when he:

1. **Calculated his DCLE:** ₹60,000 monthly.

2. **Focused on a comfortable lifestyle:** renting a cozy home and avoiding unnecessary luxury purchases.

3. **Educated himself on personal finance:** He learned about budgeting, investment strategies, and compounding growth.

4. **Invested with discipline:** Achieving a 16% annual return.

Today, Ankit's passive income is more than his DCLE, allowing him to live stress-free, travel freely, and pursue his dreams.

Now, I would like to explain how systematic investments can create a life-long passive income. By adopting a systematic investment and withdrawal strategy, you can not only cover your living expenses but also ensure your wealth grows steadily, enabling financial security for life.

The Power of Systematic Withdrawal Plans (SWP) for Passive Income

A Systematic Withdrawal Plan (SWP) can transform your investment corpus into a consistent source of passive income, ensuring you live comfortably while preserving your wealth. Here's how it works, with relatable examples:

Example 1: Building Freedom at 48

Rahul, a 48-year-old marketing professional, has built an investment corpus of ₹3 crores in equity mutual funds, earning an average annual return of 12%. His family's DCLE is ₹70,000 per month. However, to build flexibility, Rahul decides to withdraw ₹100,000 monthly and increases his withdrawal by 10% every year to keep up with inflation. Let's see how his corpus sustains:

- Initial Corpus: ₹3,00,00,000

- Monthly Withdrawal (Year 1): ₹1,00,000

- Annual Growth: 12% (average CAGR)

By the age of 80, Rahul's total corpus will have grown to ₹59.52 crores, even after total withdrawals of ₹9.79 crores over the period. His disciplined investment approach ensures a lifetime of financial security without depleting his wealth.

Example 2: Securing Retirement with SWP

Suman, aged 60, has an investment corpus of ₹5 crores in equity mutual funds with a 12% CAGR. Her DCLE is ₹1 lakh per month. She chooses to withdraw ₹1 lakh monthly, increasing this amount by 10% each year to keep pace with inflation, while keeping the remaining corpus invested for long-term wealth preservation and growth. Let's analyze:

- Initial Corpus: ₹5,00,00,000

- Monthly Withdrawal: ₹1,00,000

- Annual Growth: 12%

By the age of 80, Suman's corpus will have grown to ₹38.61 crores, even after total withdrawals of ₹4.68 crores over the period, ensuring a steady income and substantial financial growth throughout her lifetime.

Why SWPs Work for Long-Term Passive Income

1. **Tax Efficiency:** Receiving income through an SWP can be highly tax-efficient, as only a portion of the income stream is taxed as capital gains, while the remaining amount is treated as a non-taxable return of capital.

2. **Compounding Effect:** Even as you withdraw, the remaining funds continue to grow, creating a compounding effect.

3. **Flexibility:** You can adjust the withdrawal amount or frequency based on your needs.

SWPs are a practical and powerful way to enjoy financial freedom without worrying about depleting your savings.

Your Roadmap to Financial Freedom

Here's how you can start today:

1. **Calculate Your DCLE:** Determine the minimum monthly amount needed for a comfortable lifestyle.

2. **Educate Yourself:** Learn about personal finance—budgeting, debt repayment, creating income streams, and investment strategies for compounding returns of at least 12%.

3. **Create a Plan:** Develop a financial roadmap based on your DCLE and avoid distractions from FDGs.

4. **Act Consistently:** Save and invest wisely. Every small step brings you closer to financial freedom.

Once your passive income considerably exceeds your DCLE, you'll achieve ultimate financial freedom. At that point, you can work on FDGs stress-free, simply for personal satisfaction rather than out of desperation.

Conclusion

Financial freedom isn't reserved for a lucky few—it's a result of deliberate choices and actions. By focusing on what truly matters and avoiding the trap of unnecessary desires, you can create a life of peace, purpose, and prosperity.

Call to Action

Your journey begins today! Calculate your DCLE, deepen your knowledge of personal finance, and take action by investing. Stay committed to this path, and you won't just build wealth—you'll create a legacy of financial confidence and inspire others to do the same. The future you envision is within reach—start now!

Thank you

Dear Reader,

Thank you for taking the time to read this book and explore its concepts. By diving into these pages, you've taken an important step toward transforming your relationship with money and embracing a more abundant, fulfilling life. The journey to financial well-being isn't just about numbers—it's about reshaping beliefs, understanding emotions, and creating a future that aligns with your dreams.

I hope the insights and strategies in this book have inspired you to take control of your financial health and equipped you with the tools to navigate the emotional, psychological, and practical aspects of money. Remember, every small step you take today brings you closer to the financial freedom and happiness you deserve.

I am a **financial wellness coach**, **life coach**, and **investment banking** professional. I guide individuals in taking immediate control of their mental, emotional, and financial well-being. If you would like to benefit from my coaching services, please email me at **coachrajeshnawagekar@gmail.com**. Together, we can unlock your full potential and help you live your best life.

Once again, thank you for allowing me to be a part of your journey. Wishing you success, growth, and abundance in every area of your life!

Warm regards,

Rajesh Nawagekar

www.ingramcontent.com/pod-product-compliance
Lightning Source LLC
Chambersburg PA
CBHW020606160726
47991CB00002B/888